THE COOK'S COLLECTION
❋
PERFECT
PASTA

Author: Annette Wolter
Photography: Odette Teubner
Translated by UPS Translations, London
Edited by Josephine Bacon

CLB 4163
This edition published in 1995 by Grange Books
an imprint of Grange Books PLC, The Grange, Grange Yard, London SE1 3AG
This material published originally under the series title "Kochen Wie Noch Nie"
by Gräfe und Unzer Verlag GmbH, München
© 1995 Gräfe und Unzer Verlag GmbH, München
English translation copyright: © 1995 by CLB Publishing, Godalming, Surrey
Typeset by Image Setting, Brighton, E. Sussex
Printed and bound in Singapore
ISBN 1-85627-730-5

THE COOK'S COLLECTION

❊

PERFECT PASTA

Annette Wolter

Grange
BOOKS

Introduction

Originally synonymous with Italian cooking, pasta is now enjoyed widely throughout the world. The reasons for this are easy to understand: dried pasta is inexpensive, can be stored for months, and used as the basis of countless delicious meals. Its huge range of shapes and sizes, from spaghetti and tagliatelle to shells and bows, makes it extremely versatile as well as fun and interesting to eat. With fresh pasta, too, now becoming increasingly obtainable, it is even easier to create really authentic-tasting Italian dishes.

As the recipes in this book show, there are many ways to take advantage of this wonderful food. It adds texture to casseroles and stews, will enliven a salad, can be baked with a filling and creamy sauce, and it can be just as delicious cooked on its own until *al dente*, and served simply with a dribble of olive oil and a scattering of grated Parmesan cheese. Baked pasta dishes are also suitable for freezing, making them ideal for unexpected visitors.

This book describes a wonderful range of pasta dishes. Here are ideas for starters, pasta with delicious sauces, as well as bakes and salads. Whatever occasion you are cooking for, you will find inspiration within these colourful pages, and you will certainly enjoy making the dishes as much as eating them.

Each recipe serves four, unless otherwise indicated

Noodle Soup with Winter Vegetables

400g/14oz swede
200g/7oz celeriac
200g/7oz carrots
¼ head of white cabbage
1 large onion
1 tbsp oil
1l/1³/4 pints hot meat stock
100g/4oz capellini
1 tbsp finely chopped fresh parsley

Preparation time:
30 minutes
Cooking time:
25 minutes
Nutritional value:
Analysis per serving, approx:
• 920kJ/200kcal
• 7g protein
• 3g fat
• 41g carbohydrate

Wash the swede, celeriac and carrots under running cold water, peel or scrape, rinse and cut into fairly thin slices or strips. Remove the outer leaves from the white cabbage, cut out the stem, wash and cut the cabbage into strips. Peel the onion and dice finely. • Heat the oil in a large pan, add the chopped onion and cook gently until transparent, stirring frequently. Add the other vegetables, fry for a few minutes in the oil, still stirring, then pour over the meat stock. Cover the pan and simmer over a low heat for about 20 minutes. • Add the capellini, stir the soup thoroughly and cook for about 4 minutes until al dente. Garnish with the chopped parsley just before serving.

Tip: *This soup tastes even better when a tablespoon of sour cream is added to each bowl before serving.*

Tomato Soup with Quark Dumplings

2 ripe beefsteak tomatoes
20g/¾oz butter
1 tsp wholewheat flour
1 tbsp tomato purée
1l/1¾ pints hot vegetable stock
Salt and freshly ground white pepper
2 sprigs of thyme
1 sprig of rosemary
for the dumplings:
2 hard-boiled eggs
45g/1½oz butter
1 egg
2 tbsps quark or curd cheese
3 tbsps wholewheat flour
Pinch each of freshly grated nutmeg and salt

Preparation and cooking time:
40 minutes
Nutritional value:
Analysis per serving, approx:
• 1090kJ/260kcal
• 11g protein
• 19g fat
• 8g carbohydrate

Make a crossways cut in the base of the tomatoes, immerse briefly in boiling hot water, peel and remove the bases of the stalks. Chop the flesh finely. • Melt the butter, add the flour, and fry until it is golden brown. Stir in the tomato purée, then add the vegetable stock. Season the soup with the salt, pepper, thyme and rosemary; boil for 10 minutes. • To make the dumplings, peel the hard-boiled eggs, chop very finely and mash with a fork. Mix to a smooth dough with the butter, egg, quark and flour and season with the nutmeg and salt. •Dip a teaspoon into hot water and use it to form dumplings from the dough. Add the dumplings to the soup and simmer until they rise to the surface. Make sure that the soup does not boil too

Pea Soup with Flour Dumplings

1 small leek
100g/4oz carrots
1 tbsp safflower oil
200g/7oz shelled green peas
1l/1³/₄ pints hot chicken stock
for the dumplings:
1 egg
50g/2oz butter, softened
150g/5¹/₂ oz flour
¹/₂ tsp celery salt
Generous pinch each of salt
and paprika
10 fresh mint leaves

Preparation time:
15 minutes
Cooking time:
20 minutes
Nutritional value:
Analysis per serving, approx:
• 1380kJ/330kcal
• 10g protein
• 15g fat
• 39g carbohydrate

Remove the green leaf tips and the root from the leek. Cut the leek in half lengthways, wash thoroughly and cut into fine julienne strips. Scrape and trim the carrots, cut lengthways into slices and then into strips. • Heat the oil in a large pan. Fry the leek and carrot strips with the peas, then add the chicken stock. Bring to the boil, then simmer the soup for 15 minutes. • For the dumplings, mix the egg and the butter together well, using a fork. Add the flour and celery salt and knead the mixture to a smooth dough. • Dip a teaspoon into the boiling soup and use it to form dumplings from the dough. Allow the dumplings to simmer gently in the soup until they rise to the surface. • Season the soup with the salt and paprika. • Wash the mint leaves, chop finely and sprinkle over the soup.

Pasta Soup with Borlotti Beans

200g/7oz dried borlotti beans
1 small onion
2 garlic cloves
75g/3oz streaky bacon
250g/8oz ripe tomatoes
Handful of fresh parsley
4 tbsps olive oil
About 1l/1³/₄ pints meat stock
1 tsp celery salt
Generous pinch of black pepper
150g/5¹/₂ oz ditali
2 tbsps freshly grated Parmesan cheese

Soaking time:
12 hours
Preparation and cooking time:
1³/₄ hours
Nutritional value:
Analysis per serving, approx:
• 1890kJ/450kcal
• 19g protein
• 15g fat
• 59g carbohydrate

Cover the beans with twice their volume of water and soak overnight. • Cook the beans in their soaking water in a covered pan for about 1 hour, until soft, then transfer to a sieve, retaining the cooking water. • Meanwhile, peel the onion and the garlic cloves and chop finely. Dice the bacon very finely. Peel and chop the tomatoes. Wash and dry the parsley and chop finely. •Heat the oil in a large pan, then cook the onion and garlic gently until transparent. Add the bacon, parsley, tomatoes and beans, cover the pan and simmer over a low heat for about 20 minutes. • Rub half of this mixture through a sieve. Add the meat stock to the unsieved vegetables, then add enough of the water in which the beans have been cooked to make a total of 1¹/₂l/2¹/₂ pints of liquid. • Bring the soup to the boil; season with the celery salt and the pepper. • Boil the ditali in the soup until al dente, then stir in the vegetable purée using an egg whisk. Heat through and garnish with the grated Parmesan cheese before serving.

Ravioli with Spinach Filling

300g/10oz flour
2 eggs
5 tbsps walnut oil
6-8 tbsps lukewarm water
300g/10oz spinach
2 garlic cloves
100g/4oz finely minced lean beef
100g/4oz Pecorino or Parmesan cheese
2 tbsps chopped pistachio nuts
Salt and freshly ground black pepper
Pinch of grated nutmeg
3l/5¼ pints water
1 tsp each of salt and oil

Preparation and cooking time:
1¾ hours
Nutritional value:
Analysis per serving, approx:
• 2180kJ/520kcal
• 20g protein
• 21g fat
• 61g carbohydrate

Knead the flour together with the eggs, pinch of salt, 3 tbsps walnut oil and enough water to make a smooth dough. Brush the dough with oil, cover, and leave to stand for 1 hour. • Pick over the spinach, wash thoroughly and cook without adding water over a high heat for 2 minutes, then remove excess water and chop. Peel the garlic cloves, chop finely, crush and mix with the finely minced beef. Grate the cheese coarsely. Fry the minced beef in the remaining oil, cool, and then mix with the spinach, grated cheese, pistachios and seasoning. • Roll out dough into two equal portions on a floured work surface as thinly as possible. Place small dabs of the spinach mixture onto one piece of the dough, brush the spaces between them with water, lay the second piece of dough on top and press together firmly between the filling. Cut out the ravioli using a pastry wheel. Bring water to the boil, add oil and salt and cook the ravioli in the water for 5 minutes. Serve with tomato sauce and grated cheese.

Ravioli with Cheese Filling

To serve 6:

6-7 eggs
Salt
2 tbsps oil
500g/1lb 2oz flour
250g/8oz Parmesan cheese
250g/8oz Ricotta cheese
Freshly ground white pepper
Pinch of grated nutmeg
2-3l/3½-5¼ pints water
1 tsp salt
7g/3oz butter

Preparation and cooking time:
1¾ hours

Nutritional value:
Analysis per serving, approx:
• 3610kJ/860kcal
• 43g protein
• 51g fat
• 61g carbohydrate

To make the pasta dough, break 4 or 5 eggs, depending on their size, into a bowl. Add ½ tsp salt, oil and some of the flour. Stir until a thin dough is formed. Sift the remaining flour into a bowl, add the egg mixture and knead to a shiny, smooth dough.

Place the dough under an inverted bowl and leave to stand for 1 hour. • Grate the Parmesan and mix 150g/5½oz of it with the Ricotta, the remaining eggs and salt, pepper and nutmeg. • Roll the pasta dough out on a flour-covered work surface as thinly as possible (or pass through a pasta-making machine on the thinnest setting) then cut into 5cm/2-inch squares. Place a dab of the filling on each of the squares. Brush the edges with water and fold diagonally in half. • Add salt to the water, bring it to the boil, add the ravioli and cook for about 5 minutes. Remove and drain well. • Melt the butter until it turns slightly brown, stir in the remaining Parmesan and carefully coat the ravioli with the mixture.

Home-made Tagliatelle with Spinach

200g/7oz flour
2 eggs
½ tsp salt
750g/1lb 11oz young spinach
2 garlic cloves
1 tbsp oil
2 tbsp butter
1 tsp salt
Pinch of freshly grated nutmeg
Generous pinch of freshly
ground black pepper
3l/5¼ pints water
1 tsp salt
50g/2oz freshly grated
Parmesan cheese

Preparation and cooking time:
1½ hours
Nutritional value:
Analysis per serving, approx:
• 1680kJ/400kcal
• 19g protein
• 16g fat
• 44g carbohydrate

Make a dough from the flour, eggs and salt, kneading until it is firm and smooth. Shape into a ball and leave to stand under an inverted bowl for 1 hour. • Meanwhile pick over and wash the spinach, then cook gently, without added water, until tender. • Cool the spinach, squeeze out some of the water and chop finely. • Peel the garlic cloves and cut in half. Heat the oil and 1 tbsp butter in a pan. Add the garlic halves, fry until brown, then remove from the oil. Add the spinach to the oil, season with the salt, nutmeg and pepper, then cover and leave over a low heat for 5 minutes. • Roll the dough out thinly on a floured work surface, shape into a roll, cut into strips and leave for a short while to dry out a little • Add the salt to the water and when boiling vigorously add the tagliatelle. Cook for about 5 minutes until al dente. Then drain the pasta in a colander, place in a heated dish and toss in the remaining butter. • Top the pasta with the spinach and garnish with Parmesan cheese.

Tagliatelle with Nuts and Cream

2½l/4½ pints water
1 tsp salt
250g/8oz tagliatelle
200g/7oz shelled walnuts
2 garlic cloves
4 tbsps olive oil
300ml/12 fl oz sour cream

Preparation time:
15 minutes
Cooking time:
20 minutes
Nutritional value:
Analysis per serving, approx:
• 3190kJ/760kcal
• 18g protein
• 52g fat
• 55g carbohydrate

Add the salt to the water and bring to the boil. Add the pasta and cook until it is not too soft – dry tagliatelle takes about 8 minutes; fresh pasta only requires half the time. • Grind the walnuts finely. Peel the garlic cloves and slice thinly. • Heat the oil in a large pan and add the ground walnuts (reserve some for garnishing) and the slices of garlic. Fry very gently, stirring constantly. • Drain the pasta and combine with the nut and garlic mixture. Season with a little salt. • Serve the pasta very hot in a heated dish, garnished with the remaining ground walnuts. • Heat the sour cream gently, stirring all the time, without allowing it to become too hot. Serve in a separate container to be poured over the pasta.

Tip: *If calories are not a consideration, this sumptuous pasta dish from the Balkans may be served with crème fraîche instead of sour cream. A sweet variation on this dish exists, sweetened with honey or sugar instead of being seasoned with salt, and of course leaving out the garlic.*

Spaghetti with Pepper Sauce

2 fresh red chillies
1 green pepper
2 onions
1 garlic clove
1 small courgette
2 tomatoes
3 tbsps olive oil
150g/5¹/₂oz can sweetcorn
2 tbsps tomato purée
5 tbsps dry white wine
Salt and freshly ground black
pepper
Generous pinch of dried
oregano
2¹/₂l/4¹/₂ pints water
1 tbsp salt
250g/8oz spaghetti

**Preparation and cooking
time:**
1 hour
Nutritional values:
Per person about
• 1590kJ/380kcal
• 12g protein
• 9g fat
• 64g carbohydrate

Take the chillies and the pepper, remove the stalk, seeds and white pith, wash, pat dry and chop very finely. Peel the onions and dice finely. Peel the garlic clove, chop, sprinkle with salt and crush. Wash the courgette, cut off the ends and grate coarsely. Peel the tomatoes, cut into quarters and remove the base of the stalk; dice the flesh. • Heat 2 tbsps oil in a pan, add the diced onion and cook until transparent. Stir in the other vegetables and the garlic, then add the sweetcorn. Allow the vegetable mixture to simmer over a low heat for 5 minutes. • Stir the tomato purée into the wine and combine with the vegetables. Season the sauce with the pepper and the dried oregano. Add more salt if desired. • Add salt to the water and bring to the boil, adding the remaining tablespoon of oil. Cook the spaghetti for about 8 minutes or until al dente. • Serve the sauce with the pasta and, if desired, garnish with freshly grated Parmesan.

Puszta Stew

250g/8oz green peppers
500g/1lb 2oz beefsteak
tomatoes
1 carrot
1 small turnip
1 celery stalk
250g/8oz beef (prime rib)
Generous pinch of freshly
ground black pepper
2 onions
2 garlic cloves
125ml/4fl oz olive oil
1l/1³/₄ pints hot water
1 tbsp vegetable stock granules
1 tsp sweet paprika
1 tsp caraway seeds
¹/₂ tsp dried thyme
100g/4oz wholewheat fusilli
¹/₂ tsp hot paprika
1 tbsp each finely chopped fresh
parsley and chives
100g/4oz Pecorino or
Parmesan cheese

Preparation and cooking time:
1 hour
Nutritional value:
Analysis per serving, approx:
• 2180kJ/520kcal
• 19g protein
• 37g fat
• 27g carbohydrate

Cut the peppers into quarters, remove the seeds and slice the flesh into thin strips. Peel the tomatoes and dice the flesh. Peel or scrape the carrot and turnip, scrub the celery and chop them all finely. Dice the meat and sprinkle with the pepper. • Peel the onions and the garlic; dice finely. Heat the olive oil in a large heavy-based pan, add the onions and garlic and cook gently for a few minutes before removing with a slotted spoon. Fry the meat in the oil in two batches, turning until crispy brown. Add the onion and garlic and the prepared vegetables, frying for a more few minutes. Then add the water, the stock granules, the paprika, caraway and dried thyme. Cover and simmer for 10 minutes. • Add the pasta and continue to cook, without a lid, for about 8 minutes. • Stir in the paprika, parsley and chives, ensuring that the soup does not boil again. • Grate the cheese finely, and just before eating, sprinkle over the soup.

Spaghetti alla Carbonara

3l/5¼ pints water
1½ tsps salt
1 tbsp oil
400g/14oz spaghetti
50g/2oz streaky bacon
50g/2oz Pecorino or Parmesan cheese
2 garlic cloves
1 tbsp olive oil
2 eggs
4 tbsps single cream
½ tsp salt
Generous pinch of white pepper

Preparation and cooking time:
30 minutes
Nutritional value:
Analysis per serving, approx:
• 2520kJ/600kcal
• 20g protein
• 25g fat
• 74g carbohydrate

Bring the water to the boil, then add the salt, the oil and the spaghetti. Cook the spaghetti for about 8 minutes or until al dente. • Dice the bacon finely and grate the cheese. Peel and quarter the garlic cloves. • Heat the olive oil in a large pan. Add the garlic and fry for a few minutes until brown, stirring frequently, then remove and discard. Fry the diced bacon in the olive oil until it is brown and crispy. • In a warmed bowl, beat the eggs with the cream, the cheese, the salt and pepper. • Drain the spaghetti in a colander, combine with the bacon in the pan and heat through well, stirring. Mix together in the serving dish with the egg and cream mixture.

Tip: This dish tastes even better if two egg yolks are added to the cream sauce.

20

Spaghetti alla Napoletana

2 tbsps olive oil
1 onion
Sprig each of parsley and basil
400g/14oz chopped tomatoes
Pinch of hot paprika
2¹/₂ tsps salt
Pinch of sugar
3l/5¹/₄ pints water
1 tsp oil
400g/14oz spaghetti
50g/2oz Parmesan cheese

Preparation and cooking time:
40 minutes
Nutritional value:
Analysis per serving, approx:
• 2180kJ/520kcal
• 22g protein
• 13g fat
• 79g carbohydrate

H eat the oil in a saucepan. Peel the onion, dice finely and fry in the oil until golden brown. • Wash and dry the herbs, remove the tough stems, chop the leaves finely and add to the onion. • Add the chopped tomatoes to the onion. Then add the paprika, ¹/₂ tsp salt and the sugar. Cover and simmer over a very low heat for 10 minutes. • Cook the spaghetti in vigorously boiling water with the remaining salt and oil for about 8 minutes or until al dente. • Grate the Parmesan. Mix the drained spaghetti with the tomato sauce in a heated serving bowl. • Serve accompanied by grated Parmesan.

Penne with Asparagus Tips

400g/14oz canned tomatoes
1 large garlic clove
3 anchovy fillets
1kg/2¼lbs green asparagus
3 tbsps olive oil
2l/3½ pints water
1½ tsps salt
1 tsp oil
200g/7oz penne
Generous pinch of freshly
ground white pepper

Preparation and cooking time:
45 minutes

Nutritional value:
Analysis per serving, approx:
• 1380kJ/330kcal
• 15g protein
• 10g fat
• 49g carbohydrate

Drain the tomatoes in a sieve, then chop roughly. Peel the garlic clove and cut in half lengthways. Rinse the anchovies, pat dry and chop finely. • Wash the asparagus thoroughly under running lukewarm water and cut the green upper halves into pieces about 3cm/1¼ inches long (the remainder of the asparagus may be used to make a soup). • Heat the oil in a large pan. Stir the pieces of garlic, the anchovies, tomatoes and asparagus into the hot oil, then cover and cook over a low heat for about 15 minutes. • Meanwhile, add the oil and 1 tsp salt to the water and bring to a rolling boil. Add the pasta, stir once thoroughly and cook for about 8 minutes or until al dente. • Drain in a colander and place in a heated dish. • Season the vegetables with the remaining salt and the pepper before combining with the pasta. Cover and leave to stand for about 3 minutes before serving to allow the flavours to develop.

Tip: *If you are able to buy ripe, aromatic, outdoor-grown tomatoes with plenty of flavour, you should of course use them in preference to the canned variety.*

Spaghetti with Calf's Kidneys

400g/14oz calf's kidneys
400g/14oz can tomatoes
Handful of fresh parsley
1 onion
3 tbsps oil
Salt and freshly ground white
pepper
1 tsp flour
1 tbsp butter
3 tbsps Marsala or sherry
4l/7 pints water
2 tsps salt
400g/14oz spaghetti

**Preparation and cooking
time:**
1 hour
Nutritional value:
Analysis per serving, approx:
• 2600kJ/620kcal
• 32g protein
• 19g fat
• 81g carbohydrate

Cut the kidneys in half lengthways, carefully remove any skin or tubes on the inside, then soak in cold water for 30 minutes, changing the water several times. • Drain the tomatoes and chop them into small pieces. Wash and dry the parsley and chop finely. • Peel the onion and cut into thin rings. Heat the oil and fry the onion until transparent. Then add the tomatoes and season with the salt and pepper. Cook the sauce without a lid over a medium heat in order to evaporate some of the liquid. • Dry the kidneys, slice and dust lightly with flour. • Heat the butter in a separate pan, add the kidneys and fry for a few minutes until brown. Then pour over the Marsala or sherry. As soon as the wine has evaporated, add the kidneys and parsley to the tomato sauce, seasoning to taste. • Bring the water to the boil. Add the salt and the spaghetti and cook for about 8 minutes or until al dente. Drain in a colander and serve immediately with the kidneys.

Pasta with Lamb Ragout

750g/1lb 11oz shoulder of lamb
2 garlic cloves
Sprig of rosemary
3 tbsps oil
1 tbsp butter
1 tbsp tomato purée
125ml/4fl oz cup of lamb stock
Salt and freshly ground white pepper
3l/5¼ pints water
1½ tsps salt
300g/10oz tagliatelle verdi

Preparation and cooking time:
1 hour
Nutritional value:
Analysis per serving, approx:
• 3400kJ/810kcal
• 44g protein
• 45g fat
• 55g carbohydrate

Wash and dry the meat, then cut it into pieces, removing all bone. Peel the garlic cloves. Wash and dry the rosemary and remove the needles from the stem. Chop the garlic and the rosemary finely. • Heat the oil in a large heavy-based pan, add the pieces of meat and brown on all sides over a medium heat. Pour off all the cooking fat. Add the butter, garlic and rosemary. Combine the tomato purée with the stock and pour on top. Season the meat with salt and pepper. Cover the ragout and cook for 30 minutes or until the meat is tender. • Bring the water to the boil, add the salt, then the pasta, and cook for about 8 minutes or until al dente. Drain in a colander and place in a heated serving bowl with the ragout. • Serve accompanied by a fresh tomato salad.

Pasta Ragout with Mushrooms

600g/1lb 6oz oyster
mushrooms
25g/1 oz butter
Salt and freshly ground black
pepper
2 tsps paprika
3 tbsps tomato purée
150g/5¹/₂oz crème fraîche
4l/7 pints water
2 tsps salt
400g/14oz macaroni
Small handful of fresh parsley
Freshly grated Parmesan or
Emmental cheese (optional)

Preparation and cooking time:
40 minutes
Nutritional value:
Analysis per serving, approx:
- 2600kJ/620kcal
- 80g protein
- 26g fat
- 79g carbohydrate

Rinse the oyster mushrooms in cold water, pat dry, wipe and cut into pieces. • Heat the butter in a pan, add the mushrooms and cook for a few minutes before adding the salt, pepper and paprika. Mix the tomato purée with the crème fraîche and combine with the mushrooms. Leave the mixture to simmer over a low heat. • Meanwhile, add the salt to the water and bring it to the boil. Then drop in the pasta and cook for about 8 minutes or until al dente. • Wash and dry the parsley, remove the tough stems and chop the leaves finely. • Drain the pasta in a colander, then combine with the mushroom sauce in a heated dish. Garnish with parsley. • If desired, serve with freshly grated Parmesan or Emmental.

Tip: Since pasta mixed with sauce should always be served very hot, it is recommended that the serving dish be heated in a low oven while the dish is being prepared. If you do not want to use the oven, leave the serving bowl filled with very hot water until you are ready to serve. Alternatively, serve the meal straight onto attractive warmed plates.

Lamb and Apple Pasta Casserole

700g/1lb 9oz leg of lamb, boned
2 large onions
3-4 garlic cloves
5 tbsps olive oil
Salt and freshly ground black pepper
1 tsp curry powder
500ml/16fl oz hot lamb stock
1 bay leaf
500g/1lb 2oz cooking apples
3l/5¼ pints water
1½ tsp salt
300g/10oz pasta (gemelli, macaroni or fusilli)
1-2 tsps cornflour
3 tbsps finely chopped fresh parsley

Preparation and cooking time:
2½ hours
Nutritional value:
Analysis per serving, approx:
• 3690kJ/880kcal
• 43g protein
• 44g fat
• 80g carbohydrate

Cut the meat into large cubes. Peel and dice the onions. Peel the garlic and chop finely. • Heat 4 tbsps olive oil in a large heavy-based saucepan, add the meat and brown over a medium heat. Then add the onions and the garlic and fry for a few more minutes. Season with the salt, pepper and curry powder, then pour over the stock. Add the bay leaf, cover and cook over a low heat for 1½ hours. • Twenty minutes before the end of the cooking time, quarter and peel the apples, remove the cores, chop and add to the meat. • Bring the water to the boil with the salt and the remaining oil. Add the pasta and cook until al dente. • Stir a little cold water into the cornflour and use to thicken the ragout. Garnish with parsley. • Drain the pasta well and serve with the meat.

Tagliatelle Verde with Prawns

300g/10oz peeled prawns
1 tbsp lemon juice
1 small onion
2 garlic cloves
25g/1oz butter
250g single cream
150g/5½oz crème fraîche
200g/7oz freshly grated
Parmesan cheese
4l/7 pints water
2 tsps salt
1 tbsp oil
400g/14oz fresh tagliatelle
verdi
Salt and freshly ground white
pepper
1 tsp dried tarragon

Preparation and cooking time:
30 minutes
Nutritional value:
Analysis per serving, approx:
• 3990kJ/950kcal
• 38g protein
• 54g fat
• 78g carbohydrate

Rinse the prawns with cold water in a sieve, drain and sprinkle with the lemon juice. Peel the onion and dice finely. Peel and crush the garlic cloves. • Heat the butter in a large pan, add the prawns and fry for a few minutes. Then add the diced onion and the garlic and fry for a few more minutes. Pour the cream and the crème fraîche over the prawns and bring to the boil. Sprinkle over 100g/4oz Parmesan and stir into the mixture. Remove from the heat and keep warm while cooking the pasta. • Bring the water to the boil, add the salt, the oil and the pasta and cook until al dente. Drain well. • Season the prawn and cream sauce with the salt, pepper and tarragon. Serve with the pasta and the remaining Parmesan.

Spaghetti with Chicken Breasts

2 onions
2 x 250g/8oz chicken breasts
200g/7oz can sweetcorn
1 tbsp oil
250ml/8fl oz chicken stock
Generous pinch of hot paprika
4l/7 pints water
2 tsps salt
1 tbsp oil
400g/14oz spaghetti
3 tbsps chopped chives

**Preparation and cooking
time:**
40 minutes
Nutritional value:
Analysis per serving, approx:
• 2520kJ/600kcal
• 44g protein
• 8g fat
• 87g carbohydrate

Peel the onions and chop
them finely. Wash and dry
the chicken, remove the skin
and bones and cut the flesh
into small even-sized pieces.
Drain the sweetcorn. • Heat
the oil, add the chopped onion
and fry until golden. Then add
the chicken and fry until
lightly browned. Stir in the
sweetcorn, pour over the
chicken stock and add the
paprika. Cover and cook over
a low heat for 15 minutes. •
Add the salt and oil to the
water and bring to the boil,
then slide in the spaghetti and
cook for about 8 minutes or
until al dente. • Drain the pasta
thoroughly and place in a
heated serving dish. Pour the
chicken sauce over the
spaghetti, mix together well
and serve garnished with the
chives.

Tortellini with Chervil and Cheese Sauce

4l/7 pints water
2 tsps salt
1 tbsp oil
500g/1lb 2oz fresh tortellini with meat filling
1 onion
25g/1oz butter
1 heaped tbsp flour
125ml/4fl oz hot meat stock
125ml/4fl oz dry white wine
250ml/8fl oz single cream
Salt and freshly ground white pepper
Pinch of fresh grated nutmeg
200g/7oz full-fat soft cheese
100g/4oz fresh chervil
1 egg yolk

Preparation and cooking time:
30 minutes
Nutritional value:
Analysis per serving, approx:
• 2390kJ/570kcal
• 15g protein
• 15g fat
• 41g carbohydrate

Bring the water to the boil, adding the salt and oil. Drop in the tortellini and cook for about 10 minutes. • Peel the onion and chop finely. • Heat the butter, then add the chopped onion and fry gently for a few minutes. Sift the flour over the onion and brown lightly before gradually adding the stock. Stirring constantly, bring the sauce to the boil. • Stir in the wine and the cream and bring back to the boil. Season with the salt, pepper and nutmeg. Chop the cheese roughly, add to the sauce and melt over a low heat. Wash the chervil, remove any tough stems, chop and stir into the sauce. • Mix the egg yolk with 2 tbsps of the sauce, then stir the mixture into the sauce to thicken it. • Drain the tortellini well and combine with the sauce.

Chow Mein

12 dried black mushrooms
(mu err)
3l/5¼ pints water
1½ tsps salt
300g/10oz Chinese egg
noodles
400g/14oz fillet of pork
1-2 tbsps cornflour
3 tbsps soya sauce
3 spring onions
2 carrots
1l/1¾ pints oil for frying
250g/8oz canned or fresh
bean sprouts
4 tbsps oil

**Preparation and cooking
time:**
1 hour
Nutritional value:
Analysis per serving, approx:
• 2600kJ/620kcal
• 33g protein
• 25g fat
• 69g carbohydrate

Cover the mushrooms with lukewarm water and leave to soak. • Add salt to the water and bring to the boil. Place the egg noodles in the water and boil for about 6 minutes. Then pour into a colander, rinse with cold water and drain on a kitchen towel. • Cut the fillet of pork into strips 1cm/½ inch thick. Coat with cornflour and then dip into 1 tbsp soya sauce. • Trim the onions and slice them into rings. Peel or scrape the carrots and slice thinly. • Heat the frying oil in a deep-fat fryer or frying pan to 180°C/350°F. Add the noodles in batches, frying each until crispy brown, then drain on absorbent paper and keep warm. •Heat the oil in a pan, add the strips of meat and stir-fry for 2 minutes. Then add the sliced carrot and the onion rings. Rinse and drain the bean sprouts if canned, add to the pan and stir-fry the whole mixture for another 3 minutes. • Add the mushrooms and their soaking liquid to the meat, together with the remaining soya sauce, and cook for a further 2 minutes. Season the mixture with some more soya sauce. Thicken, if necessary, using 1 tsp cornflour mixed with a little cold water. • Serve with the noodles.

Swiss Cheese Noodles

150g/5¹/₂oz Emmental cheese
2 large onions
375g/12oz flour
125ml/4fl oz water
2 eggs
2¹/₂ tsps salt
4l/7 pints water
50g/2oz butter

Preparation and cooking time:
45 minutes

Nutritional value:
Analysis per serving, approx:
• 2810kJ/670kcal
• 25g protein
• 28g fat
• 75g carbohydrate

Grate the cheese. Peel the onions and slice them into thin rings. Sift the flour into a bowl. Combine with the water, the eggs and ¹/₂ tsp salt, briskly kneading into a soft but firm dough. Add more flour or water as required. Add the remaining salt to the water and bring to the boil. Divide the dough into small portions and place them one by one on a dampened wooden board. Flatten slightly and, using a long knife, slice off very thin strips, dropping them into the boiling water. Alternatively, the tiny noodles (spaetzle) may be made by pressing the dough through a wide-meshed sieve. When cooked the spaetzle will float to the surface. • Remove the spaetzle from the water using a slotted spoon, drain in a colander and keep hot. • Melt the butter in a large pan, add the onion rings and fry until golden brown. • Place the spaetzle in layers in a heated dish with the cheese and top with the onion rings.

Austrian Noodles with Cabbage

250g/8oz flour
2 eggs
Pinch of salt
1 onion
1 small head of cabbage (about
500g/1lb 2oz)
3 tbsps oil
1 tbsp sugar
Just under 125ml/4fl oz hot
vegetable stock
Freshly ground black pepper
3l/5¼ pints water
1½ tsps salt
1 tbsp oil

**Preparation and cooking
time:**
1¾ hours
Nutritional value:
Analysis per serving, approx:
• 1590kJ/380kcal
• 12g protein
• 12g fat
• 58g carbohydrate

Knead the flour with the eggs, the salt and a little water, if needed, into a smooth dough. Place under an inverted bowl and leave to stand for 1 hour. • Meanwhile, peel the onion and slice into thin rings. Remove the outer leaves from the cabbage. Cut into quarters, wash, remove the hard core and cut the leaves into thin strips. • Heat the oil in a large heavy-based pan. Add the onion rings and fry until golden brown; sprinkle over the sugar and allow it to caramelize. Add the cabbage, continue frying for a few minutes, then pour over the stock, season with the pepper, cover and simmer for 30 minutes. • Meanwhile roll the dough out very thinly on a work surface and cut into 4cm/1½-inch squares. Leave to dry for a few minutes. • Bring the water to the boil, add the salt and the oil, then drop in the squares and cook for about 4 minutes. When cooked, drain them in a colander, combine with the cabbage and leave for a few minutes for the flavours to blend.

Bami Goreng

3l/5¼ pints water
1½ tsps salt
300g/10oz udon (Japanese wheat flour noodles) or thin spaghetti
300g/10oz chicken breast fillets
250g/8oz Chinese leaves
4 spring onions
3 celery stalks
1 small fresh chilli
2 garlic cloves
5 tbsps oil
250g/8oz peeled prawns
Just under 250ml/8fl oz chicken stock
2 tbsps soya sauce

Preparation and cooking time:
45 minutes
Nutritional value:
Analysis per serving, approx:
• 2310kJ/550kcal
• 40g protein
• 14g fat
• 63g carbohydrate

Add salt to the water and bring it to the boil. Add the noodles, stir once thoroughly and cook for about 8 minutes or until al dente. • Meanwhile wash and dry the chicken breast fillets and cut them into 1cm/³/₈-inch thick strips. • Drain the noodles in a colander. • Remove the outer leaves and base from the Chinese leaves, wash, pat dry and cut into strips. Remove the root and tough leaves from the spring onions, wash and slice into rings. Wash and dry the celery, remove any tough threads and slice thinly. Wash the chilli, dry, cut in half, remove the stem, any pith and the seeds and dice finely. Peel the garlic cloves and chop finely. • Heat 4 tbsps oil in a wok or deep pan, add the chicken and fry for 2 minutes, browning all over. Then remove it from the oil.

Combine the chopped vegetables, place them in the oil and stir-fry for 5 minutes. Mix in the prawns and the chicken strips, add the chicken stock and the soya sauce,

cover, and simmer over a low heat for a few more minutes. • Reheat the noodles in the remaining oil in another pan. • Combine the vegetables with the noodles.

37

Potato Gnocchi

1 kg/2¼lbs floury potatoes
150g/5½oz Parmesan cheese
250-300g/8-10oz flour
4l/7 pints water
Salt
100g/4oz butter
Sprig of flat-leaved parsley

Preparation and cooking time:
1¼ hours
Nutritional value:
Analysis per serving, approx:
• 3400kJ/810kcal
• 25g protein
• 40g fat
• 92g carbohydrate

Peel and rinse the potatoes, cut into equal-sized pieces, cover with salted water and boil for about 20 minutes. • Grate the Parmesan. • Mash the potatoes and leave to cool. Sprinkle them with a little salt, then knead them together with enough flour to make a smooth, not too firm dough. • Leave the dough to stand for 10 minutes, then divide into 8 portions and roll each portion into a strand about 2cm/½ inch thick. Cut into 2.5cm/1-inch lengths and flatten each piece slightly with a fork, leaving a ridged surface. • Put the water in a large saucepan, add 2 tsps salt and bring to the boil. Add the gnocchi and stir gently with a fork. They will float to the surface when cooked. • Use a slotted spoon to remove and drain the gnocchi. Grease the inside of a very hot dish with a generous amount of the butter, and melt the remainder • Place the gnocchi in layers in the dish, sprinkling the grated Parmesan and the melted butter over alternate layers. • Serve immediately, sprinkled with chopped parsley.

Polenta Gnocchi

1¼l/2¼ pints water
1 tbsp salt
350g/11oz coarsely ground
polenta or cornmeal
100g/4oz Parmesan cheese
100g/4oz butter, melted
150ml/5fl oz single cream
Butter for greasing

Preparation and cooking time:
1 hour

Nutritional value:
Analysis per serving, approx:
• 3190kJ/760kcal
• 18g protein
• 44g fat
• 70g carbohydrate

Place the water in a large saucepan and bring to the boil. Add the salt, then slowly add the polenta, stirring with an egg whisk so that no lumps form. Cook the polenta over a low heat for about 45 minutes, stirring occasionally. A solid paste will form. • Meanwhile, grate the Parmesan. Grease a shallow heatproof dish with a generous amount of butter. • Shape the gnocchi from the polenta with a tablespoon dipped in hot water and layer them in the dish. Sprinkle the Parmesan over the first layer, spread the melted butter over the second layer, and finally, pour the cream over the top layer. • Place the dish under a preheated grill for about 5 minutes to reheat and brown the top.

Pasta Bake with Mushrooms

250g/8oz pasta (macaroni or spirale)
2¹/₂ l/4¹/₂ pints water
1 tsp salt
250g/8oz broccoli
250g/8oz mushrooms
2 tbsps oil
1 garlic clove
2 eggs
250ml/8fl oz milk
Pinch each of salt, paprika and grated nutmeg
125g/5oz grated Parmesan cheese
1 tbsp each flaked almonds, sesame seeds and melted butter

Preparation time:
30 minutes
Baking time:
40 minutes
Nutritional value:
Analysis per serving, approx:
• 2600kJ/620kcal
• 32g protein
• 29g fat
• 57g carbohydrate

Cook the pasta in salted water until al dente. • Wash the broccoli. Slice the stems finely, leaving the florets whole. Wipe the mushrooms and slice them finely. Peel the garlic. • Heat 1 tbsp oil and fry the garlic clove briefly. Add the broccoli and cook over a low heat, stirring frequently, for 3 minutes. Then remove from the pan. • Add the remaining oil to the pan. Add the mushrooms and cook until golden . • Drain the pasta. • Heat the oven to 225°C/ 425°F/Gas Mark 7 and butter an ovenproof dish. • Place alternate layers of pasta, broccoli and mushrooms in the dish. Separate the eggs. Beat the egg yolks with the milk, salt, paprika, nutmeg and Parmesan. • Whisk the egg whites until they are fairly stiff, then fold them in. • Pour the egg mixture into the dish. Sprinkle with almond leaves and sesame seeds. Drip melted butter over the top and bake for about 40 minutes.

Bucatini and Aubergine Bake

To serve 6:
3 aubergines
1 tbsp salt
400g/14oz bucatini
4l/7 pints water
1 bunch spring onions
2 carrots
150g/5½ oz celery
Sprig of thyme
125ml/4fl oz olive oil
800g/28oz can tomatoes
100g/4oz grated Feta cheese
150g/5½oz Mozzarella cheese

Preparation time:
1 hour
Baking time:
30 minutes
Nutritional value:
Analysis per serving, approx:
• 3480kJ/830kcal
• 24g protein
• 40g fat
• 91g carbohydrate

Cut the aubergines into slices 1cm/½ inch thick, coat with salt and leave to stand for 20 minutes. • Break the pasta into pieces and cook until al dente. • Peel the onions and carrots, wash the celery and chop all finely. Chop the thyme leaves finely. Heat 2 tbsps oil in a large pan and fry the vegetables gently. • Break up the tomatoes and add them to the vegetables together with their juice. Boil for a few minutes to reduce the liquid. • Heat the oven to 220°C/425°F/Gas Mark 7. •Rinse the sliced aubergine with cold water and pat dry. Heat the remaining oil in a separate pan and fry the aubergine until brown, then drain off any remaining oil. • Butter a large ovenproof dish and put in half the bucatini. Stir in 2 tbsps of the grated cheese and pour over the tomato sauce. Arrange the aubergine slices on top, then add the remaining bucatini, followed by another layer of aubergine. • Cover with thin slices of Mozzarella and bake for 30 minutes.

Luxury Pasta

1 small onion
1 garlic clove
150g/5¹/₂oz fillet of pork
100g/4oz streaky bacon
100g/4oz ceps or button
mushrooms
50g/2oz butter
1 tbsp brandy
125ml/4fl oz single cream
Salt and freshly ground black
pepper
4l/7 pints water
2 tsps salt
400g/14oz tagliatelle
75g/3oz freshly grated
Parmesan cheese

**Preparation and cooking
time:**
40 minutes
Nutritional value:
Analysis per serving, approx:
• 3610kJ/860kcal
• 31g protein
• 48g fat
• 76g carbohydrate

Peel the onion and the garlic and dice finely. Rinse the meat briefly with cold water, pat dry and cut into strips. Dice the bacon finely. Wipe, rinse, dry and slice the mushrooms. • Heat the butter in a pan. Add the onion and garlic and fry until golden brown. Then add the meat, bacon and mushrooms and cook through. Pour over the brandy, and when the liquid has evaporated, pour in the cream. Season the mixture with salt and pepper, cover, and continue to cook over a low heat. • Meanwhile bring the water to the boil, add the salt and the pasta and cook the pasta until al dente. Drain well. • Combine the meat ragout, the pasta and the Parmesan. Serve immediately.

Cut Noodles with Beans

100g/4oz wheatmeal flour
1 tbsp yeast extract
1/2 tsp ground caraway seeds
Sea salt
3 eggs
500g/1lb 2oz French beans
200g/7oz mushrooms
2 onions
50g/2oz butter
4 tbsps single cream
Freshly ground black pepper
100g/4oz Bresaola (Italian
smoked beef), thinly sliced
2l/3½ pints water
1 tsp salt
2 tbsps finely chopped parsley
100g/4oz grated Gruyère
cheese

Preparation time:
1½ hours
Baking time:
15 minutes
Nutritional value:
Analysis per serving, approx:
• 1800kJ/430kcal
24g protein
• 31g fat
13g carbohydrate

To make the cut noodles, mix the flour thoroughly with the yeast extract, caraway seeds, 2 generous pinches of salt and the eggs. Cover and leave to stand. • Meanwhile wash and trim the beans, break them into pieces and cook in a little water for 20 minutes. Wipe the mushrooms and slice finely. • Peel the onions, dice finely, and fry in 40g/1¼oz butter until transparent. Add the mushrooms, the remaining salt, the cream and the pepper; cook for 10 minutes. • Cut the smoked meat into strips 1cm/½ inch wide. • Heat the oven to 200°C/400°F/ Gas Mark 6. • Add salt to the water and bring it to the boil. Make the spaetzle by scraping small pieces from the dough and cooking them in the water until they float to the surface. • Drain the beans and mix them with the spaetzle, the mushrooms, the strips of meat and the parsley. Place the mixture in a buttered ovenproof dish, sprinkle with the cheese, and dot with the remaining butter. Bake for 15 minutes.

Wholewheat Pasta with Fennel

500g/1lb 2oz Florence fennel
250g/8oz wholewheat
macaroni
2¹/₂l/4¹/₂ pints water
1 tsp salt
4 eggs
250ml/8fl oz single cream
2 tbsps wholewheat flour
6 tbsps tomato purée
2 generous pinches each of
garam masala and white pepper
2 tsps celery salt
4 tbsps finely chopped parsley
50g/2oz butter
200g/7oz Gouda or Edam
cheese

Preparation time:
25 minutes
Baking time:
30 minutes
Nutritional value:
Analysis per serving, approx:
• 3480kJ/830kcal
• 36g protein
• 50g fat
• 58g carbohydrate

Wash the fennel, chop off the root and the tops, cut into quarters lengthways and then crossways into thin slices. Retain some of the green leaves. Cook the pasta with the fennel in vigorously boiling salted water for about 8 minutes, so that the pasta is al dente, then pour into a colander, rinse briefly with cold water and drain. • Beat the eggs with the cream, flour, tomato purée, spices and 2 tbsps chopped parsley. • Heat the oven to 180°C/350°F/Gas Mark 4 and butter an ovenproof dish . • Place the pasta and fennel in the dish, pour over the cream and egg mixture and bake for 20 minutes. •Slice the cheese thinly and lay on top, then dot with the remaining butter. Bake for a further 10 minutes. • Chop the fennel leaves finely. Garnish the dish with the remaining parsley and the fennel leaves before serving.

Pasta Tomato Bake

250g/8oz tagliatelle
21/2/²/₂ pints water
1 tsp salt
1 bulb florence fennel
3 tomatoes
Handful of mixed fresh herbs
(chervil, tarragon, dill and sage)
3 tbsps butter
125ml/4fl oz single cream
100g/4oz cooked lean ham
150g/5¹/₂oz crème fraîche
125ml/4fl oz milk
2 eggs
Salt and freshly ground white
pepper
2 tbsps breadcrumbs

Preparation time:
30 minutes
Baking time:
20-30 minutes
Nutritional value:
Analysis per serving, approx:
• 3310kJ/790kcal
• 25g protein
• 46g fat
• 70g carbohydrate

Cook the pasta in vigorously boiling salted water until al dente. Chop the root and top off the fennel and retain some of the leaves. Slice the fennel and then cut into very thin strips. Slice the tomatoes thickly. Wash and dry the herbs and the fennel leaves, then chop them finely. Heat 1 tbsp of the butter and fry the strips of fennel; then add the cream and chopped herbs. Dice the ham finely and stir into the mixture. • Heat the oven to 200°C/400°F/ Gas Mark 6. Grease an ovenproof dish with 1 tbsp butter. • Fill the dish with alternate layers of the drained pasta, the fennel mixture and the tomatoes. • Beat the eggs with the crème fraîche and the milk, season with salt and pepper and pour over the dish. Top with the breadcrumbs and dabs of the remaining butter. • Bake for 20-30 minutes.

Lasagne with Spinach

700g/1lb 9oz spinach
500ml/16fl oz water
Salt
50g/2oz butter
50g/2oz flour
250ml/8fl oz milk
Pinch each of grated nutmeg
and freshly ground white
pepper
100g/4oz full fat soft cheese
100g/4oz Pecorino or
Parmesan cheese
2 large beefsteak tomatoes
250g/8oz lasagne
2½l/4½ pints water
1 tsp salt
1 tbsp oil
½ tsp dried oregano

Preparation time:
45 minutes
Baking time:
30 minutes
Nutritional value:
Analysis per serving, approx:
• 2600kJ/620kcal
• 24g protein
• 27g fat
• 67g carbohydrate

Pick over the spinach, removing coarse stems, wash it thoroughly and blanch in boiling salted water for 2 minutes. Drain, retaining the cooking water. • Heat the butter in a small pan. Add the flour and cook until golden, stirring constantly, then gradually add the milk and enough spinach water to make a creamy béchamel sauce. Season with the nutmeg and pepper, then stir in the cream cheese in small dabs. • Coarsely grate the Pecorino or Parmesan. Wash, dry and slice the tomatoes. • If cooking is required, cook the pasta in batches in boiling salted water, to which oil has been added, until al dente, then drain. •Heat the oven to 200°C/400°F/ Gas Mark 6. Oil an oven dish , place a layer of pasta in the bottom, and cover it with a layer of spinach, then a layer of tomato slices. Sprinkle with dried oregano and grated cheese. Cover with a thin layer of béchamel sauce. Repeat the same procedure, finishing with a generous amount of sauce. • Cook the lasagne on the middle shelf of the oven for 30 minutes.

Bucatini Timbale

250g/8oz wholewheat flour
¹/₂ tsp salt
100g/4oz butter
1 egg
1kg/2¹/₄lbs tomatoes
3 garlic cloves
4 tbsps olive oil
2 tsps each finely chopped
fresh basil and marjoram
Generous pinch of black pepper
200g/7oz wholewheat bucatini
2l/3¹/₂ pints water
1 tsp salt
75g/3oz black olives
150g/5¹/₂oz Parmesan or
Pecorino cheese
1 tbsp butter

Preparation time:
50 minutes
Baking time:
40 minutes
Nutritional value:
Analysis per serving, approx:
• 3900kJ/930kcal
• 32g protein
• 53g fat
• 78g carbohydrate

Sift the flour into a bowl with the salt, rub in the butter and bind together with the egg. Shape the pastry into a ball, cover and put in the refrigerator. • Peel and dice the tomatoes. Peel the garlic cloves and chop finely. Heat the oil in a large pan and fry the garlic until transparent. Add the tomatoes, herbs and pepper and cook for 15 minutes until most of the liquid has evaporated. • Meanwhile break the bucatini into pieces and cook in salted water for about 8 minutes; then drain in a colander. • Stone the olives and dice them finely. Grate the cheese finely. Stir the pasta, the olives and the cheese into the tomato mixture. • Butter an ovenproof dish and heat the oven to 180°C/350°F/ Gas Mark 4. • Roll the pastry out thinly and line the dish. Add the filling and cover with a pastry lid, pressing the edges down firmly. Make a hole in the centre of the pastry and decorate with pastry trimmings. Top with dabs of butter. • Bake the timbale for 40 minutes until golden brown.

Pasta Pizza

To serve 8:
500g/1lb 2oz spaghetti
5l/8³/₄ pints water
2 tsps salt
2 green peppers
200g/7oz salami, sliced thinly
500g/1lb 2oz tomatoes
8 eggs
350ml/14fl oz milk
1 tbsp cornflour
100g/4oz grated Parmesan cheese
2 tsps each Italian mixed herbs, paprika and finely chopped basil
1 tsp salt
300g/10oz Emmental cheese
About 4 tbsps olive oil
2 tbsps chopped chives

Preparation time:
40 minutes
Baking time:
30 minutes
Nutritional value:
Analysis per serving, approx:
• 2940kJ/700kcal
• 37g protein
• 40g fat
• 41g carbohydrate

Cook the pasta in salted water for 8 minutes. • Cut the peppers into quarters lengthways, cut out the stem and the pith and remove the seeds. Cut the flesh crossways into fine strips. Add to the pasta for the last 2 minutes of cooking time. Drain both in a sieve, rinse briefly and drain. • Butter two ovenproof dishes. Heat the oven to 180°C/350°F/Gas Mark 4. Divide the pasta mixture between the dishes, then place the slices of salami on top. Wash the tomatoes, cut them into thin slices and arrange on top of the salami. Beat the eggs with the milk, the cornflour, the Parmesan and the seasonings and pour over the tomatoes. Grate the Emmental coarsely and sprinkle onto the tomatoes, then pour the olive oil over the top. • Bake for about 30 minutes, and serve garnished with chives.

Pasta with Pesto

2 handfuls of fresh basil
2-3 garlic cloves
1 tbsp pine kernels
Pinch of salt
100g/4oz freshly grated
Parmesan cheese
250ml/8 fl oz cold-pressed
extra-virgin olive oil
4l/7 pints water
2 tsps salt
400g/14oz pasta (spaghetti,
bucatini or fettuccine)
1 tbsp butter

**Preparation and cooking
time:**
30 minutes
Nutritional value:
Analysis per serving, approx:
• 3400kJ/810kcal
• 23g protein
• 47g fat
• 74g carbohydrate

Wash the basil and remove the leaves from the stems. Peel the garlic cloves, chop, and crush together with the basil, pine kernels and the salt, using a pestle and mortar, until a smooth paste is formed. Stir in the Parmesan. Add the oil, initially drop by drop, and then in a thin stream, stirring it into the paste. • Bring the water to the boil, then add the salt and the pasta. Boil the pasta until al dente, then rinse in a colander with warm water, drain and toss in the butter. • Serve the pesto as an accompaniment to the pasta.

Tip: Pesto may be made in advance and stored. It may be kept in a refrigerator, covered with olive oil, and placed in a sealed jar, for at least a week.
The flavour of the pesto may be varied by replacing half of the basil with parsley and using ground almonds in place of pine kernels.

Neapolitan Baked Bucatini

2 aubergines
2 tsps salt
500g/1lb 2 oz tomatoes
1 onion
1 carrot
1 celery stalk
Small handful of fresh basil
6 tbsps olive oil
Salt and freshly ground black pepper
250g/8oz bucatini
2½l/4½ pints water
1 tsp salt
100g/4oz freshly grated Parmesan or Pecorino
200g/7oz Mozzarella

Preparation time:
1¼ hours
Baking time:
20–30 minutes
Nutritional value:
Analysis per serving, approx:
• 2680kJ/640kcal
• 27g protein
• 33g fat
• 60g carbohydrate

Wash and slice the aubergines, sprinkle with salt and leave to stand for 30 minutes. • Peel the tomatoes and chop finely, removing the bases of the stalks. • Peel the onion and the carrot and clean the celery. Remove the basil leaves from their stems, wash and pat them dry. Chop all the vegetables and the basil finely. • Heat 2 tbsps olive oil in a large pan and cook the vegetables over a low heat for a few minutes, then add the tomatoes and season with salt and pepper. Continue to cook over a medium heat until the mixture thickens. • Rinse the aubergine slices, pat dry and fry in batches in the remaining oil. Drain on absorbent paper when cooked. •Break the bucatini into pieces and cook in the salted water until al dente, then rinse and drain. •

Heat the oven to 220°C/ 425°F/Gas Mark 7. Butter an ovenproof dish thoroughly. • Liquidize or sieve the sauce. Mix the pasta with half the sauce and all the grated cheese. Place half of this mixture in the oven dish and cover with

50

the aubergine slices. Arrange
thin slices of Mozzarella on
top. Then add the remaining
pasta, aubergines and
Mozzarella in consecutive
layers. Pour over the
remaining sauce. • Bake in the
oven for 20-30 minutes.

Baked Pasta Turkish Style

3l/5¼ pints water
1 tsp salt
300g/10oz bucatini or
macaroni
50g/2oz butter
3 tbsps flour
500ml/16fl oz milk
3 eggs
Freshly ground white pepper
50g/2oz chopped walnuts
50g/2oz freshly grated
Pecorino or Parmesan cheese

Preparation time:
35 minutes
Baking time:
30 minutes
Nutritional value:
Analysis per serving, approx:
• 2680kJ/640kcal
• 23g protein
• 31g fat
• 68g carbohydrate

Bring the water to the boil, then add the salt and the pasta. Cook for 10 minutes or until al dente, then pour into a colander, rinse briefly with cold water and drain. • Melt the butter in a saucepan over a low heat, add the flour and cook, stirring, until golden. Gradually pour in the milk, stirring constantly. Simmer the sauce for about 10 minutes, then remove from the heat and allow to cool a little. • Heat the oven to 200°C/400°F/Gas Mark 6. • Beat the eggs with the pepper and stir into the sauce. • Butter an oven dish, pour in some of the sauce, arrange the pasta on top and sprinkle with the nuts. Then pour over the rest of the sauce and sprinkle the cheese on top. • Bake for 30 minutes until golden brown. • Serve hot, cut into portions. • A tomato salad with onion rings and black olives would go well with this dish.

Onion and Bucatini Bake

2¹/₂l / 4¹/₂ pints water
1 tsp salt
250g / 8oz bucatini
1kg / 2¹/₄lbs Spanish onions
1 garlic clove
3 tbsps oil infused with herbs
Salt and freshly ground black
pepper
4 eggs
100ml / 3fl oz sour cream
2 tbsps finely chopped fresh
parsley
100g / 4oz freshly grated
Emmental cheese
2 tsps paprika

Preparation time:
1 hour
Baking time:
30 minutes
Nutritional value:
Analysis per serving, approx:
• 2680kJ / 640kcal
• 27g protein
• 29g fat
• 67g carbohydrate

Bring the water to the boil, then add the salt and the pasta. Cook for 10 minutes or until al dente, then pour into a colander, rinse with cold water and drain. • Peel the onions and cut into thin rings. Peel the garlic clove and chop finely. • Heat the oil in a large pan. Add the onion rings and garlic and fry for a few minutes. Then cook, uncovered, over a high heat for about 10 minutes so that some of the liquid can evaporate, stirring occasionally. Season with the salt and pepper. •Beat the eggs with the cream, then stir in the parsley, the grated cheese and the paprika. • Heat the oven to 200°C / 400°F / Gas Mark 6. Butter an ovenproof dish. •Put a layer of onions on the bottom, then add a layer of bucatini, followed by another layer of onion. Pour over the cream mixture. • Bake for 30 minutes until crispy and golden brown.

Russian Pasta au Gratin with Quark

2½l/4½ pints water
250g/8oz fettuce (short-cut ribbon pasta)
1 tsp salt
3 tbsps oil
200g/7oz streaky bacon
2 onions
1/2 tsp dried marjoram
500g/1lb 2oz quark or curd cheese
2 eggs
125ml/4fl oz single cream
Freshly ground white pepper
75g/3oz butter
4 tbsps breadcrumbs
2 tbsps finely chopped fresh parsley

Preparation time:
35 minutes
Baking time:
40 minutes
Nutritional value:
Analysis per serving, approx:
• 4620kJ/1100kcal
• 35g protein
• 74g fat
• 64g carbohydrate

Bring the water to the boil, then add the pasta, the salt and 1 tsp oil. Cook the pasta until it is al dente, then pour it into a colander and drain well.
• Cut the bacon into thin strips. Peel the onions and dice finely. Heat the remaining oil in a pan and fry the strips of bacon and the diced onion until golden brown. Stir in the pasta and the marjoram. • Mix the quark or curd cheese in a bowl with the eggs and the cream, seasoning generously with salt and pepper. • Heat the oven to 180°C/350°F/Gas Mark 4. Butter an ovenproof dish. • Arrange a third of the pasta in the dish, spread half the quark mixture over the top, then add another layer of pasta, followed by the rest of the quark mixture and top with the remaining pasta. Heat the remaining butter in a small pan, remove from the heat and stir in the breadcrumbs. Spread over the pasta. • Bake on the middle shelf of the

54

oven for about 30 minutes.
Then turn the heat up to
250°C/475°F/Gas Mark 9,
move the dish to the top shelf
and bake for another 10
minutes to brown the top. •
Serve garnished with the
parsley.

Amsterdam Pasta Salad

250g/8oz pasta shapes
2¹/₂l/4¹/₂ pints water
1 tsp salt
4 hard-boiled eggs
6 small tomatoes
1 small cucumber
1 red pepper
200g/7oz corned beef
Salt and freshly ground white pepper
Generous pinch garlic powder
Pinch sugar
2 tbsps cider vinegar
3 tbsps oil infused with herbs
Small handful of fresh parsley

Preparation time:
40 minutes
Marinating time:
30 minutes
Nutritional value:
Analysis per serving, approx:
• 2010kJ/480kcal
• 29g protein
• 17g fat
• 53g carbohydrate

Cook the pasta in the salted water for 8-10 minutes or until al dente, then rinse briefly in a colander with cold water, drain and leave to cool. • Shell the eggs and cut them into quarters. Wash, dry and quarter the tomatoes, removing the bases of the stalks. Wash and slice the cucumber, then cut the slices in half. Halve the pepper, remove the stalk, seeds and pith, wash and dice finely. Cut the corned beef into thin strips. •Combine the salt, pepper, garlic powder and sugar, then stir into the oil and vinegar. •Gently mix the pasta with the vegetables, corned beef and pieces of egg. Dress the salad with the oil and vinegar, cover and leave to marinate at room temperature for 30 minutes. • Wash the parsley, chop finely and use to garnish the salad just before serving.

Danish Pasta Salad

2½l/4½ pints water
1 tsp salt
1 tsp oil
250g/8oz pasta shapes
300g/10oz frozen peas and carrots
Salt and freshly ground black pepper
2 pineapple rings
1 pickled gherkin
250g/8oz cooked lean ham, unsliced
200g/7oz mayonnaise
3 tbsps lemon juice
2 tbsps pineapple juice
3 tbsps milk
½-1 tsp curry powder

Preparation time:
30 minutes
Cooling time:
1 hour
Nutritional value:
Analysis per serving, approx:
• 3100kJ/740kcal
• 26g protein
• 44g fat
• 62g carbohydrate

Bring the water to the boil, then add the salt, oil and pasta. Cook the pasta until al dente, pour into a colander, rinse and drain thoroughly. • Place the peas and carrots in a pan containing 4 tbsps water, salt and pepper. Bring the water to the boil, cover, and cook for 4 minutes over a low heat, then allow to cool. • Cut the pineapple into neat pieces. Dice the gherkin and the ham. •Mix the mayonnaise with the lemon juice, pineapple juice and milk. Season with the curry powder and a pinch of salt. • Combine the pasta with the other ingredients and the dressing. Cover and stand in a cool place for 1 hour, then add more seasoning if required.

Indian Pasta Salad

2l/3½ pints water
1 tsp salt
6 tbsps oil
200g/7oz tagliatelle
4 chicken breast fillets
1 tsp ground coriander
2-3 tsps curry powder
Generous pinch of white pepper
4 tbsps Marsala or sweet sherry
100g/4oz almonds
2 bananas
1 tbsp lemon juice
2 tbsps raisins
4 tbsps light soy sauce

Preparation time:
1 hour
Marinating time:
2 hours
Nutritional value:
Analysis per serving, approx:
• 2680kJ/640kcal
• 46g protein
• 28g fat
• 47g carbohydrate

Bring the water to the boil. Add the salt, 1 tsp oil and the pasta. Cook the pasta until it is al dente, then pour into a colander and drain well. • Rub ½ tsp coriander, 1 tsp curry powder, a generous pinch of salt and the pepper into the chicken. Heat 2 tbsps oil, then brown the chicken breast fillets over a high heat. After a few minutes, pour over the Marsala, cover and cook over a low heat for 5 minutes. Leave the chicken to cool in the sauce. •Blanch the almonds, remove the skins and roast them in a dry pan until golden brown. Peel and slice the bananas and sprinkle them with lemon juice. Wash the raisins in hot water and pat them dry. Then cut the chicken into 3cm/1¼- inch pieces. • To make the dressing, mix ½ tsp coriander with 2 tsps curry powder, the soy sauce, a pinch of salt and 4 tbsps oil. • Gently stir the pasta, the chicken with its juice, the sliced banana, almonds and raisins into the dressing. Leave to stand in a cool place for at least 2 hours. •Season again before serving.

Arabian Pasta Salad

400g/14oz rigatoni
4l/7 pints water
1 tsp salt
1 cucumber
425g/15oz jar of sweet-sour pickled squash
100g/4oz feta cheese
Small handful of dill
Juice of ½ lemon
1 tbsp concentrated apple juice
150ml/5½ oz yogurt
1 tbsp mayonnaise
5 mint leaves
2 tbsps sesame seeds

Preparation time:
20 minutes
Marinating time:
30 minutes
Nutritional value:
Analysis per serving, approx:
• 2100kJ/500kcal
• 19g protein
• 12g fat
• 81g carbohydrate

Cook the pasta for about 8 minutes or until al dente, then rinse briefly with cold water in a colander, drain and allow to cool. • Dice the cucumber, together with the drained squash. Crumble the cheese. Wash the dill, pat dry and chop finely. • Mix the lemon juice with the concentrated apple juice, the yogurt, mayonnaise and dill. • Wash the mint leaves, pat dry and cut into strips. Combine the pasta with the diced cucumber and squash, the cheese and mint. Dress the salad with the yogurt sauce and leave to marinate for 30 minutes. • Meanwhile dry-fry the sesame seeds, stirring frequently, until golden brown. Leave to cool. • Serve the pasta salad garnished with the sesame seeds.

Tagliatelle Salad with Red Lentils

50g/2oz dried figs
50g/2oz dried apricots
150g/5¹/₂oz red lentils
500ml/16fl oz water
1 bay leaf
2 tsps vegetable stock granules
2l/3¹/₂ pints water
1 tsp salt
200g/7oz wholewheat tagliatelle
50g/2oz Bresaola (Italian smoked beef)
50g/2oz dates
200g/7oz sour cream
2-3 tbsps lemon juice
Freshly ground white pepper
1 tbsp finely chopped fresh parsley

Preparation time:
45 minutes
Marinating time:
15 minutes
Nutritional value:
Analysis per serving, approx:
• 2100kJ/500kcal
• 20g protein
• 11g fat
• 81g carbohydrate

Wash the figs and the apricots, blanch in a small bowl with boiling hot water, cover, and leave to soak. • Add the lentils, the bay leaf and the vegetable stock granules to the water, bring to the boil and cook over a low heat for just under 10 minutes. • Cook the pasta in boiling salted water for about 10 minutes or until al dente. • Drain the lentils and the pasta respectively in a sieve (removing the bay leaf from the lentils), rinsing both briefly with cold water. • Cut the Bresaola into thin strips. Drain the soaked dried fruit and cut into strips. Stone the dates and cut into strips. Mix the sour cream in a bowl with 2 tbsps lemon juice and the pepper.

Then stir in the chopped and cooked ingredients, together with the parsley. Season with more lemon juice and pepper

if required. • Cover and leave
to marinate at room
temperature for about 15
minutes before serving.

Pasta Salad with Herb Cream Sauce

200g/7oz gnocchi or conchiglie
2l/3½ pints water
1 tsp salt
125ml/4fl oz oil
500g/1lb 2oz red peppers
200g/7oz canned tuna
2 small onions
5 hard-boiled eggs
176g/6oz mixed fresh herbs
(borage, dill, tarragon, chervil,
lovage, parsley, sorrel, lemon
balm)
1 garlic clove
1 tbsp mustard
4 tbsps yogurt
Salt and freshly ground white
pepper
100g/4oz stoned green olives

Preparation time:
1 hour
Marinating time:
2 hours
Nutritional value:
Analysis per serving, approx:
• 2310kJ/550kcal
• 23g protein
• 29g fat
• 47g carbohydrate

Cook the pasta in salted water containing 1 tbsp oil for about 8 minutes or until al dente, then drain and allow to cool. • Remove seeds, pith and stalks from the peppers and cut the flesh into thin strips. Drain the tuna fish well and break into pieces. Peel the onions and slice into fine rings. • Halve the eggs, mash the yolks and combine with the remaining oil. (Keep the whites for another dish or meal.) Wash and dry the herbs, chop them finely with the garlic, then stir into the egg yolk mixture, together with the mustard and yogurt. Season with salt and pepper. • Combine the sauce with the pasta, the strips of pepper, onion rings, tuna fish and olives. • Leave to stand in a cool place for 2 hours.

Pasta Verde Salad

200g/7oz tagliatelle verde
2l/3¹/₂ pints water
1 tsp salt
1 tsp oil
250g/8oz small courgettes
500g/1lb 2oz asparagus
8 tbsps olive oil
Salt and freshly ground black pepper
75g/3oz streaky bacon
3 spring onions
1 garlic clove
4 tbsps vinegar
1 tsp capers
3 tbsps chopped parsley
1 tbsp chopped basil
Pinch of sugar
1 tbsp grated Parmesan cheese

Preparation time:
1 hour
Marinating time:
1 hour
Nutritional value:
Analysis per serving, approx:
• 1890kJ/450kcal
• 15g protein
• 23g fat
• 48g carbohydrate

Cook the pasta in salted water, containing 1 tsp oil until it is al dente, then drain in a colander. • Trim and wash the courgettes and asparagus; slice the courgettes thinly. Heat 2 tbsp of the olive oil in a large frying pan and cook the courgettes for 5 minutes. Remove from the pan, season with salt and pepper, then leave to cool. • Cut the asparagus into pieces, cook in a little salted water for 10-15 minutes, then drain. • Add 1 tbsp oil to the frying pan, dice the bacon finely and fry until cooked. • Cut the onions into thin rings. • Peel and crush the garlic clove and combine with the vinegar, salt and pepper, the capers, parsley, basil, sugar and Parmesan. Stir in the remaining 5 tbsps oil. •Mix the vegetables with the bacon, pasta and vinaigrette. • Leave the salad to marinate for 1 hour.

Index